SCHOLASTIC discover more™

Dolphins

By Penelope Arlon
and Tory Gordon-Harris

Contents

Literacy Consultant: Barbara Russ, 21st Century Community Learning Center Director for Winooski (Vermont) School District

Natural History Consultant: Kim Dennis-Bryan, PhD

Library of Congress Cataloging-in-Publication Data Available

ISBN 978-0-545-62738-2

10 9 8 7 6 5 4 3 2 1   14 15 16 17 18

Printed in Malaysia   108
First edition, January 2014

Diving dolphins

Have you seen dolphins leap and flip in the water? There are 42 kinds of dolphin, all smart and graceful.

Big and small

The orca, also known as the killer whale, is the biggest dolphin. It can be 32 feet (9.8 m) long!

The smallest dolphin is the Maui's dolphin, at about 4 feet (1.2 m) long. It lives off the coast of New Zealand.

male human

Kinds of dolphin

spinner dolphin

spotted dolphin

bottlenose dolphin

common dolphin

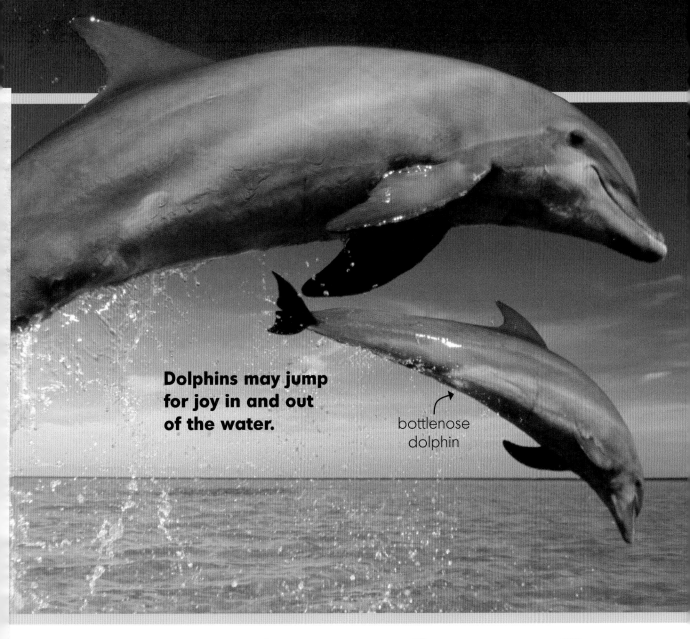

Dolphins may jump for joy in and out of the water.

bottlenose dolphin

dusky dolphin

false killer whale

Hector's dolphin

Commerson's dolphin

Water mammals

Dolphins look like fish, but they are actually mammals that live in water.

All mammals breathe air. Dolphins swim to the ocean's surface to breathe.

blowhole

Like most mammals, dolphins give birth to live young and make milk to feed them.

A dolphin breathes air through its blowhole, not through its mouth.

Mammals are warm-blooded animals. Their bodies can keep warm in cold water.

Dolphins can close their blowholes underwater.

Sleepyhead

A dolphin doesn't really sleep! It can rest one half of its brain while the other half keeps the dolphin breathing and alert for danger.

zZ
z

Super senses

Dolphins are smart animals. They have strong senses, to find out about the world around them, and big brains.

Supersmart

Dolphins have large brains for their body size, which suggests that they are very intelligent. They have bigger brains than humans do!

dolphin brain

human brain

Dolphins make sounds that bounce off prey and echo back to them. This is called echolocation.

squid (a
favorite snack)

Most dolphins have
very good eyesight,
both in the water
and out of it.

Dolphins have thick
but sensitive skin. They
often use touch to
"talk" to one another.

Dolphins cannot smell,
but they can taste. They
have favorite foods just
like we do!

A dolphin finds food by
using echolocation.

Speedy swimmers

A dolphin's body is perfectly designed for living and moving underwater.

Look inside

A dolphin's bones are spongier than a land animal's bones are. This makes the dolphin light so that it doesn't sink! Its skin is ten times thicker than yours is, with a blubbery layer that keeps it warm.

Dolphins can swim five times faster than the fastest human swimmer can!

With strong thrusts of its tail, a dolphin can "stand" out of the water.

The tail flicks up and down to move the dolphin along.

The dorsal fin on its back keeps a dolphin from rolling over.

Life in a pod

Dolphins live in groups called pods or schools. Pod members work together and teach the young.

Pods can combine to form superpods. This superpod is porpoising, or traveling in short leaps.

Pods normally have 15–20 members.

The members help one another find food.

Females help look after newborn calves.

Danger!

The great white shark and the orca are most dolphins' greatest enemies. Dolphins fight sharks off by ramming them from below with their snouts.

If a dolphin is injured, pod members help it.

They call to one another with clicks and whistles.

They play and enjoy one another's company.

Baby care

Baby dolphins, called calves, are born underwater. They can swim as soon as they are born.

Mothers and older calves teach the babies how to hunt and play.

Babies stay close to Mom.

A calf is born and is pushed by its mother to the surface to breathe.

When Mom needs to feed, young female babysitters look after the calf.

A calf will suckle, or drink its mother's milk, for at least 18 months.

When a female dolphin is about 8 years old, she can have her own babies.

delicious octopus

After 6 months, the mother teaches the calf how to hunt for food on its own.

15

Getting along

Dolphins have their own language. They chat with one another using clicks, squeaks, and whistle-like sounds.

Every bottlenose dolphin has its own sound. The other pod members call to it by making that sound, as if it's a name.

Dolphins show off and attract one another's attention by breaching, or leaping in the air.

Dolphins like to touch one another, just like humans give handshakes and hugs.

Unlike most animals, dolphins know who their friends are and can recognize themselves in mirrors.

Dolphin sounds are among the loudest animal noises in the ocean!

Let's play!

Dolphins love to play. They splash around with one another just like we do in a pool.

These dolphins are surfing the waves for fun!

Dolphins play chase. One dolphin races after another, then rolls over it!

A piece of seaweed is perfect for a game of catch! Dolphins use all sorts of sea objects as toys.

Dolphins can make air bubbles by breathing out underwater. Then they play with the bubbles!

Like us, dolphins have different personalities. Some are show-offs, while some are quite shy.

Eat up!

Dolphins are carnivores—they eat only meat. They are skillful hunters. Few animals dare attack them.

Dolphins pop their heads out of the water to look around. This is called spy-hopping, and it can help them spot food.

Favorite dolphin snacks

squid

anchovies

crab

mackerel

Up to 220 small, sharp teeth are excellent for grabbing slippery fish and squid.

Dolphins swallow prey whole, or shake it to break it up.

Hunting in packs

Dolphins sometimes hunt alone, but they are much more successful when they hunt together as a pod.

A pod of dolphins swims around a school of fish, forcing it into a tight ball.

sponge

Pod members share hunting tricks. They use sponges to protect their snouts from sharp rocks!

These bottlenose dolphins are chasing fish toward the shore. Fish are easier to catch in shallow water.

When the fish are under control, the dolphins take turns snapping them up.

Some dolphins work with fishers by chasing fish into nets. In return, they get a meal.

Giant orcas

The most successful hunter in the ocean is the biggest dolphin, the orca.

Orcas have up to 52 teeth, each about 4 inches (10 cm) long!

Icy waves

Penguins and seals may think that they are safe on floating icebergs. But clever orcas bob up and down nearby, making waves that flip their prey off!

hungry orca

Even big animals are orca prey.

sperm
whales

penguin

seal

These giants can almost beach themselves to grab seals on land.

unlucky
seal

River life

Three kinds of dolphin swim in freshwater rivers.

Dolphins in the Amazon River in South America may be pink!

River dolphins are smaller than ocean dolphins, but their snouts are longer.

They can't see well in muddy water, so they rely on echolocation to hunt.

River dolphins live alone or in small groups.

River dolphins have few enemies. But sometimes a huge anaconda will catch an Amazon River dolphin.

Dolphins and us

Dolphins and humans have had a special friendship for thousands of years.

In ancient times, dolphins were seen as protectors of the seas. Legends from all over the world tell of dolphins rescuing ships lost at sea.

Dolphins can show us when they are sad, happy, or excited.

The greatest danger for dolphins is getting caught in fishing nets.

But humans are also dolphins' biggest threat.

Overfishing takes food away from dolphins. Dirty river water has caused some kinds of dolphin to disappear.

But there's good news for dolphins, too! A new kind, the Burrunan dolphin, was recently found in Australia.

Glossary

beach (verb)
To become stranded on land.

blowhole
The opening, or pair of openings, in the top of a dolphin's head that allows it to breathe.

blubber
The layer of fat under the skin of a dolphin, whale, or seal.

breach (verb)
To leap out of water and into the air.

calf
The young of some animals, such as dolphins, cows, and elephants.

carnivore
An animal that eats meat.

dorsal fin
The fin on a dolphin's back.

echolocation
A way that an animal can find food and other objects in the dark or underwater. The animal makes sounds that bounce off the objects and echo back to the animal.

freshwater
Water that contains no salt, or very little salt. Most rivers are freshwater, while oceans are salty.

iceberg
A large piece of freshwater ice that floats in the sea.

mammal
A warm-blooded animal. Mammals

breathe air and feed milk to their young. Humans and dolphins are mammals.

overfishing
Taking too many fish out of the sea, so that not many are left.

pod
A group of some sea animals, such as dolphins or whales, that swim and feed together. Two or more pods can combine to make a very large superpod.

porpoise (verb)
To travel through water by making short leaps into the air.

prey
An animal that is hunted by another animal as food.

snout
The long front part of an animal's head. A dolphin's snout includes its mouth and jaws.

spy-hop (verb)
To stick the head out of the water. Dolphins spy-hop to look around or find food.

suckle (verb)
To drink milk from a female animal.

threat
Something that is a danger to something else.

warm-blooded
Having a warm body temperature that does not change. Mammals are warm-blooded. Their body temperatures stay the same even when their surroundings change.

Index

Thank you

Art Director: Bryn Walls
Designer: Ali Scrivens
Managing Editor: Miranda Smith
Managing Production Editor: Stephanie Engel
US Editor: Esther Lin
Cover Designer: Neal Cobourne
DTP: John Goldsmid
Photo Editor: Marybeth Kavanagh

Photography and artwork credits

1: blickwinkel/Alamy Images; 2tr: Paul Airs/Alamy Images; 3: iStockphoto/Thinkstock; 4–5 (dolphins leaping): Mike Hill/Alamy Images; 4 (orca): MichaelPrice/iStockphoto; 4 (Maui's dolphin): Jon Hughes; 4bl, 4bcl: iStockphoto/Thinkstock; 4bcr: MichaelPrice/iStockphoto; 4br: jamenpercy/iStockphoto; 5bl: ad_doward/iStockphoto; 5bcl: Protected Resources Division, Southwest Fisheries Science Center, La Jolla, California/Wikipedia; 5bcr: James Shook/Wikipedia; 5br: Kirsten Wahlquist; 6–7 (dolphins with fish): Stephen Frink Collection/Alamy Images; 6 (smiling dolphin): Paul Airs/Alamy Images; 7tl: anthonycake/iStockphoto; 7tc: serengeti130/iStockphoto; 7tr: aragami123345/iStockphoto; 7br: urosr/iStockphoto; 8–9 (dolphin hunting): Image Source/Alamy Images; 8 (brains): Boksi/State Museum of Natural History Stuttgart/Wikipedia; 8 (octopus): Tammy616/iStockphoto; 9tl: ViewApart/iStockphoto; 9tc: szgogh/iStockphoto; 9tr (background): Peter Schinck/Fotolia; 9tr (squid): Dansin/iStockphoto; 10–11 (dolphin swimming): blickwinkel/Alamy Images; 10bl: Thierry Berrod, Mona Lisa Production/Science Source; 11tr: brightstorm/iStockphoto; 11cr: Becart/iStockphoto; 11bl: vixdw/iStockphoto; 12–13 (superpod): DavidMSchrader/iStockphoto; 12bl: A7880S/Shutterstock; 12bc: Willyam Bradbery/Shutterstock; 12br: DebraMcGuire/iStockphoto; 13tr: Michael Patrick O'Neill/Science Source; 13bl: Gennadiy Poznyakov/Fotolia; 13bc: skynesher/iStockphoto; 13br: Angus/Fotolia; 14: Willyam Bradbery/Shutterstock; 15tr: skynesher/iStockphoto; 15ct: DebraMcGuire/iStockphoto; 15cl: Jeff Kinsey/Fotolia; 15cr: Antonio_Husadel/iStockphoto; 15cb: Tammy616/iStockphoto; 16–17 (dolphins talking): Frans Lanting, Mint Images/Science Photo Library/Science Source; 17tr: Fuse/Thinkstock; 17cr: Aleksandr Lesik/Fotolia; 17br: Nichols801/iStockphoto; 18–19 (dolphins surfing): blickwinkel/Alamy Images; 18bl: Aleksandr Lesik/Fotolia; 18br: George Karbus Photography; 19bl: Angel Fitor/Science Photo Library/Science Source; 19br: emilywineman/iStockphoto; 20: iStockphoto/Thinkstock; 21tl (background): Peter Schinck/Fotolia; 21tl (squid): Lunamarina/iStockphoto; 21tcl: Nikontiger/iStockphoto; 21tcr (background): crisod/Fotolia; 21tcr (crab): JustineG/iStockphoto; 21tr (background): Peter Schinck/Fotolia; 21tr (mackerel): PicturePartners/iStockphoto; 21b: Alexis Rosenfeld/Science Photo Library/Science Source; 22–23 (dolphins hunting): Christopher Swann/Science Photo Library/Science Source; 23 (sponge): AndreasReh/iStockphoto; 23tr: Janet Mann, National Academy of Sciences/AP Images; 23cr: czardases/Fotolia; 23br: Timothy Allen; 24–25 (orca hunting): Wildlife GmbH/Alamy Images; 24bl: Wikipedia; 24tr: wwing/iStockphoto; 25tl: Gabriel Barathieu/Flickr/Wikipedia; 25tc: flammulated/iStockphoto; 25tr: Photoart-Sicking/Fotolia; 26–27 (Amazon River dolphin): Mark Carwardine/Peter Arnold/Getty Images; 27tl: dennisvdw/iStockphoto; 27tc: Dennis Otten/Wikipedia; 27tr: Mark Smith/Science Source; 28–29 (dolphin and swimmer): Alexis Rosenfeld/Science Photo Library/Science Source; 28bl: iStockphoto/Thinkstock; 29tl: SteveDF/iStockphoto; 29cr: Mark Carwardine/Minden Pictures; 29br: Adrian Howard/Monash University, School of Biological Sciences; 30–31: iStockphoto/Thinkstock.

Cover credits

Front cover: (tr) iStockphoto/Thinkstock; (tl) hdere/iStockphoto; (dolphins l, c) Stephen Frink/Getty Images; (dolphin r) Brandon Cole Marine Photography; (water) AndreyKuzmin/Dreamstime; (splash) Emevil/Dreamstime; (background icon) Bluedarkat/Dreamstime. Back cover: (computer monitor) Manaemedia/Dreamstime.